Le

Feeling Awful

THE INSIDE STORY

Illustrated by Christopher Masters

PICCOLO
PAN MACMILLAN
CHILDREN'S BOOKS

Also by Lesley Newson in Piccolo

BURGERS AND BUGS
THE SCIENCE BEHIND FOOD

First published 1979 by A. & C. Black Ltd
This Piccolo edition published 1991 by
Pan Macmillan Children's Books Ltd,
Cavaye Place, London SW10 9PG
1 3 5 7 9 8 6 4 2
Text © Lesley Newson 1979
Illustrations © Christopher Masters 1979
ISBN 0 330 31989 2
Printed in England by Clays Ltd, St Ives plc

Contents

Diseases

Like most people you probably feel all right most of the time, but once in a while you notice that something is wrong: a headache, a stomach ache, a sore throat or you just feel tired and miserable. Often the feeling goes away of its own accord, but sometimes it gets worse and other things start to happen.

Your nose starts running, your ears hurt, you get spots. This probably means you have a disease. And all those feelings are the symptoms of the disease.

Each type of disease produces a certain set of symptoms and sometimes you can identify the disease by the kind of symptoms it causes (this is called diagnosing). Once you know what the disease is, you often know what to expect next and how long it's going to last.

A disease may have many symptoms, but doctors and scientists have found that usually they have only one cause. To cure a disease, you have to get rid of the cause. The body is good at doing this itself, and for some diseases there are medicines that help the body to cure the disease. In other diseases medicines help to get rid of the symptoms so that you don't feel so awful while you wait for the body to cure itself.

Germs

Many diseases are caused by living organisms, often referred to as "microbes" or "germs". These are usually either *bacteria* or *viruses*, organisms so small that it takes a powerful microscope to see them. There are millions of them living around and inside us all the time. Some types are harmful to us, others helpful and some do not affect us at all.

SOME GERMS

HARM US ...DON'T AFFECT US ...HELP US

Bacteria

Bacteria make milk go sour and food go bad but other kinds of bacteria turn milk into yoghurt and kitchen waste into useful compost for the garden. There are bacteria inside us that help digest our food but others that cause sore throats, ear-ache, whooping cough, pneumonia and pimples.

The thing that makes bacteria most dangerous to the body is their remarkable ability to multiply. If they have food (and the body is a lovely rich place for bacteria – warm, moist and full of food), they reproduce. Each bacterium eats and grows until it has doubled in size and then it splits in two. Some do this every twenty minutes.

If a single bacterium of this kind began to feed and reproduce at 8 a.m., there would be two of them by 8.20 a.m. By 8.40 a.m. there would be four. By 2.20 p.m. there would be 524 288 and twenty minutes later there'd be over a million. If you looked carefully you might be able to

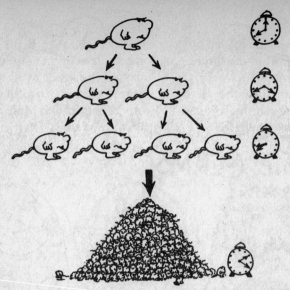

see them. The whole cluster of a million bacteria would be about the size of a pinprick. If you lined them all up, end to end, the line would be about 25 mm long, but it would be much too thin to see. By 8 p.m. at night the cluster would be much bigger and would contain nearly 70000 million bacteria.

Bacteria have huge appetites. They have to eat a lot in order to reproduce so quickly. When disease-causing bacteria live in your body, they not only eat the food in your body that was meant for you, they also eat you.

Bacteria don't have mouths or stomachs, so they can only eat things that are dissolved in water. When they eat you, the bacteria first release poisons that kill the tiny part of the body they occupy. Then they release chemicals to digest that part of the body. The chemicals break down your tissues into small bits of food. This food is then taken inside the bacterium through tiny holes in its skin.

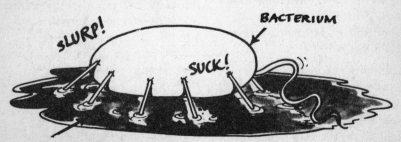

SLURP!

BACTERIUM

SUCK!

FOOD DISSOLVED IN WATER

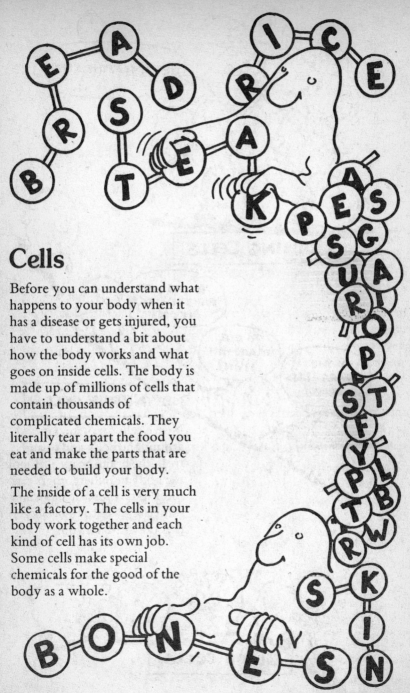

Cells

Before you can understand what happens to your body when it has a disease or gets injured, you have to understand a bit about how the body works and what goes on inside cells. The body is made up of millions of cells that contain thousands of complicated chemicals. They literally tear apart the food you eat and make the parts that are needed to build your body.

The inside of a cell is very much like a factory. The cells in your body work together and each kind of cell has its own job. Some cells make special chemicals for the good of the body as a whole.

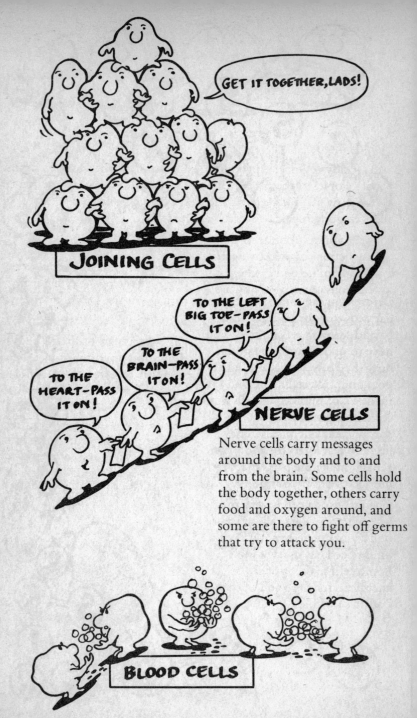

Nerve cells carry messages around the body and to and from the brain. Some cells hold the body together, others carry food and oxygen around, and some are there to fight off germs that try to attack you.

8

CELL DIVIDING

Many body cells can reproduce – make copies of themselves. This is how the body grows and keeps in good repair.

All this work is done according to instructions carried by nearly every cell in the body. The instructions are in code and are stored in a special chemical scientists call deoxyribonucleic acid or DNA for short. (Biologists cracked the DNA code about thirty years ago.) Every living organism has DNA, which carries the information necessary for making that organism.

The DNA in each of the cells in your body contains the instructions necessary to make a person who would look just like you. Identical twins look alike because their DNA is coded in exactly the same way. Even though every cell in the body has its own job they all contain the same instructions. Somehow they know which instruction they must follow.

Scientists are now able to make alterations in DNA. This 'genetic engineering' could one day make it possible to repair damage in the DNA in order to treat incurable genetic diseases.

An experiment on frog's eggs shows the importance of DNA: scientists replaced the DNA in the eggs of an ordinary green frog with DNA from a cell in the foot of a special white frog. The egg hatched into a tadpole and then grew into a perfect white frog and looked nothing like the frog that had laid the egg.

Viruses

Viruses aren't cells. In fact some biologists argue that they aren't even alive. Viruses are about a million times smaller than bacteria and they can't really do anything for themselves. Bacteria can at least swim around and eat. Viruses don't even do that. Inside the body they are carried around in the blood. Outside, they travel in tiny water droplets from a sneeze or cough. They are often carried in food and water. Some can pass from one person to another when people touch each other. Viruses can only reproduce when they get inside cells and, when they get inside cells, they often cause disease.

Viruses are little packets of information. Their insides are usually just DNA or a similar information-carrying molecule. Surrounding the DNA is a protective coat. This contains chemicals that help the virus stick to the outside of a cell and then enter it.

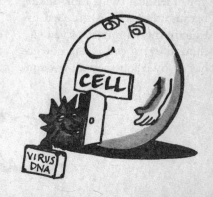

Once inside, the DNA of the virus can stop the cell's machinery from following the instructions of its own DNA and make it follow the instructions of the virus.

Some types of viruses immediately make the cell start producing hundreds of new viruses. These all burst from the cell and go to attack other cells. Sometimes this kills the cells, sometimes it only weakens them. There are other types of viruses that enter cells and stay there for a while before they begin to reproduce (see *Cold sores*, page 20). Others can change the cell slightly once they get inside (see *Warts*, page 22). And some just stay inside the cell and seem to do nothing.

Scientists are just beginning to understand how different kinds of viruses take over the body's cells. They are working to develop medicines that will help stop or slow down a virus attack.

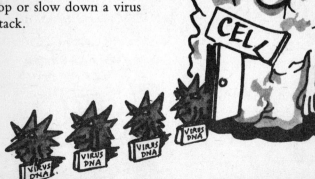

The battle to fight disease

After reading about how bacteria and viruses go about destroying you and your cells, you may be wondering how you have managed to live this long. It is because your body is defended by many different types of cells and chemicals (called the "immune system") that are always working together to fight diseases.

The immune system is very complicated and scientists still don't understand it completely. But it has been found that some of the symptoms of the most common diseases are actually caused by the immune system itself as it fights the disease.

When bacteria or viruses that infect humans fall into a wound, a pore in the skin or a tiny crevice in the throat, they can begin to reproduce and cause damage. As soon as one of your body cells is killed or wounded, it releases chemical signals that make extra blood flow to the wounded area. The signals also attract cells and chemicals of the immune systems that are always floating around in the blood.

These cells and chemicals seem to be programmed to recognize the shape of all the substances that belong inside the body because they almost always attack any foreign ones.

There are cells and chemicals of the immune system stationed round your body all the time, ready to fight off germs. But it is often necessary to call in reinforcements. To do this, a defence cell in the blood goes up to the invading germ and picks up some of the foreign chemicals surrounding it. It then carries these chemicals to some of the nearby outposts of the immune system, the lymph glands.

A lymph gland contains hundreds of defence cells. When a foreign chemical is brought to them, some of the cells are specially programmed to recognize and destroy the invaders which carry that chemical. Sometimes they go out themselves to kill the invaders and sometimes they produce chemicals called antibodies which stick to the foreign chemicals and mark them for destruction. This triggers a chain reaction with other chemicals in the blood and, in less than a second, all these chemicals working together tear apart the germ. (Scientists still aren't sure how this is done.)

Once your body contains defence cells programmed to destroy a particular germ, there is little chance of its infecting you again. The special defence cells keep patrolling the blood, destroying these invaders as soon as they enter the body. This is why you get chicken pox only once and it is how vaccinations work.

Vaccinations

When your blood contains defence cells that can recognize and destroy the germ that causes a disease, you are "immune" to the disease. Getting the disease is one way of becoming immune to it – but for serious diseases, this is definitely not the best way. Today you can "get immunized" against dangerous diseases like smallpox, diphtheria and polio with a simple injection or "vaccination".

The doctor injects you with a specially prepared sample of the bacteria or viruses that cause the disease. They have been killed or weakened so that they can't cause the disease but they still carry the foreign chemicals of the dangerous germ. The immune system prepares the specially programmed cells that can destroy the dangerous germ immediately.

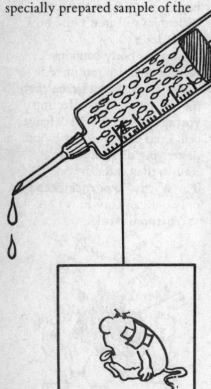

When a new type of germ enters the body, it is a few days before the blood contains defence cells that are specially programmed to destroy it. In the meantime, less effective defence strategies are used against it. A healthy germ can cause a lot of damage during this time, but the dead or weak germs used in vaccination can do no harm. They just prepare your defence system for a real attack. The swollen and sore arm you sometimes get after a vaccination is caused by the immune system fighting the harmless germs.

Colds and flu

You know what a cold is like. Your throat hurts, you cough, you can't breathe properly, you may have a headache and probably feel tired or weak for a day or two. The flu feels much the same but worse. Colds and flu are both caused by viruses that live in the breathing passages of the nose and throat. But each is caused by a different type of virus.

Cold and flu viruses attack in almost the same way. Some people get such bad colds, it seems as if they have flu, but usually the flu-virus infection feels worse. No one is sure why this is. Both diseases usually begin with a sore throat because the viruses have been reproducing inside the cells there. The cells are injured and the throat becomes red, swollen and painful as extra blood flows to the area and fluid collects there to repair the damage and kill the viruses.

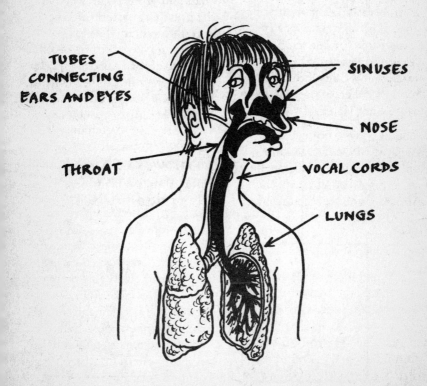

TUBES CONNECTING EARS AND EYES

SINUSES

NOSE

THROAT

VOCAL CORDS

LUNGS

The viruses get into the blood and travel around the body but seem to do little harm anywhere except in the breathing passages. They spread into many of the cells in the walls of the throat – down to the lungs, up into spaces called sinuses that lie behind the cheeks and forehead, and into the nose and the tubes that connect the nose with the eyes. These become red and swollen too as the body fights the viruses. The irritation makes you sneeze or cough.

The swelling in the nose blocks the channels the air travels through. This prevents you from breathing through your nose. The sinuses are partly responsible for our sense of smell and taste so when they are swollen it is difficult to enjoy food. Swollen sinuses can also cause a headache.

You may have noticed a swelling of a different kind when you have a cold, the flu or other diseases that attack the throat. If you feel the top of your neck on each side, you will notice small lumps there. These are swollen lymph glands.

When you have an infection in one part of the body, the nearby lymph glands often grow bigger as they increase defence production. The tonsils, two almond-shaped glands in the throat, also produce defensive cells and chemicals to protect the breathing passages and they swell up during the infection too. And they can become infected themselves (see page 29).

While the defence system is fighting viruses in the breathing passages, dead defence cells and viruses, as well as any cells that have been killed by the viruses, are falling off the walls of the passages. To get rid of this debris, the special cells that produce mucus begin to make it in extra large quantities.

Mucus is the slimy liquid that coats and protects the walls of the breathing system and the digestive system. The extra mucus you have during a cold serves to absorb the dead matter and, when you cough, sneeze or blow your nose, it carries it out of your breathing passages.

PHEW! I'VE HAD ENOUGH OF THIS!

Many scientists believe that the tired achey miserable feeling you get from a cold may be caused by another of the body's defensive strategies against the cold. Since viruses reproduce inside body cells, they reproduce much more quickly if the cells are in good condition. So the body makes the cells work more slowly and inefficiently.

One way it seems to do this is by making the temperature inside your body go up. This makes you feel quite uncomfortable. Your body works best at about 37°C (98.6°F) and, if the temperature gets much higher than this, you feel tired and miserable. But it is worse for the viruses. The high temperature slows down their reproduction rate so the defence system can get rid of them more quickly.

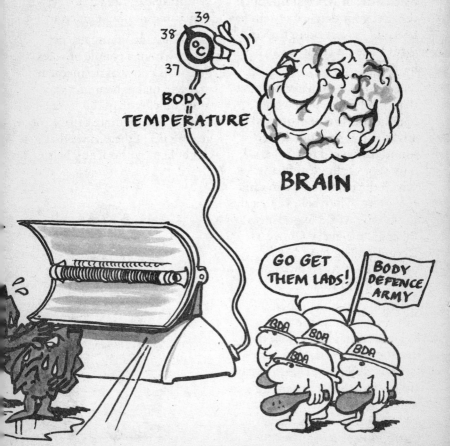

Colds and flu are the most common human diseases because we can get them more than once. This is because there are over a hundred different types of viruses that cause colds. After you've had a cold, you are immune to that particular cold virus. It will never give you a cold again. But other cold viruses will. If your best friend has a cold and you don't catch it, it may be because you are already immune to that particular virus. Or it might be because your defence system has been able to get rid of the cold virus before it could do any harm.

There are not so many viruses that cause flu so, once you've had the flu, you're protected for a while. But scientists have found that every few years a new type of flu virus forms which the defence system can't recognize. They believe that this is why the world experiences a flu epidemic every few years. Recently there have been outbreaks of Asian flu, Hong Kong flu and Red flu.

Scientists have examined the viruses that cause these epidemics and found that they are almost identical but have a slightly different protective coat. Since the defence system has not encountered the new protective coat before, it doesn't have antibodies to recognize it.

Sometimes the viral attack is unsuccessful. You will not get the flu but you will be immune to the virus. After a flu epidemic, almost everyone is immune to the virus so very few people get the flu until a new flu virus forms. Many scientists think that the old virus doesn't die out completely. It may be able to live inside the cells of other animals. After twenty years many more people will have been born. They will not be immune to the virus so it may cause another epidemic.

Colds and the flu usually get better within a couple of weeks. Scientists know of no medicine that will make them go away more quickly than this. The body is usually quite capable of getting rid of the viruses that cause them without any help.

18

But a virus infection can make it easier for bacteria to grow in your body, so it is a good idea to rest, keep warm and eat nutritious food during the worst part of the cold so your body will be able to fight any bacteria. (By the way, even though most people believe that getting cold and wet will make you catch cold, there is no scientific evidence to show that this is true.)

There are medicines you can take while you have a cold that will make you feel better. Paracetemol tablets will lower a high temperature and relieve the uncomfortable feeling. Cough syrup and sweets soothe your throat and certain kinds can help you cough up the mucus in your throat and lungs. These taste nice and some people find them helpful, but they shouldn't be taken too often.

Diseases that cause spots

The most common spot-causing diseases are chicken pox, measles and German measles. Most people get at least one of these diseases when they are children. Each one is caused by a different virus. Having measles gives you immunity to the virus that causes it but doesn't protect you from other spot-causing diseases.

These diseases are easily spread from person to person because the viruses that cause them are very good at attacking. Once a few of them enter your body, there is a good chance you will get the disease if you haven't already had it.

The viruses that cause measles usually enter the body through the nose and throat like cold and flu viruses and at first they attack in much the same way. Many of the early symptoms of measles are similar to the first symptoms of a cold and the body fights the disease as it does a cold.

But soon red splotches begin to appear on the skin. This is because the measles viruses have entered cells just underneath the surface of the skin and begun to reproduce there. This injures the cells and, just like the virus-infected cells of the throat, they release chemicals that bring extra blood and body fluids to the area to fight the virus and repair the damage. The place where the virus has attacked become red and swollen just like an infected throat.

Spots from diseases like chicken pox and German measles are caused the same way as measles spots. The viruses that cause chicken pox are called herpes

SPOT

BODY DEFENCE ARMY

virus and belong to the same type as the viruses that cause cold sores.

They can often enter the body through the skin and are seldom able to reproduce in any cells except skin cells. That is why you usually don't get any cold-like symptoms when you have chicken pox. Another way that herpes viruses are different is that they often kill the skin cells when they have finished reproducing inside them. This is why chicken-pox spots (and cold sores) are more angry and painful than measles spots.

There are no medicines to make these diseases – or the spots they cause – go away any faster than

they do naturally. But there are some quite useful medicines to put on the spots to stop them from itching so much.

Cold sores

After a person has had chicken pox he is immune to chicken pox. But scientists have found that chicken-pox viruses and other types of herpes viruses can stay in the body inside the nerve cells. They don't reproduce inside the cell or harm it in any way. They become sleeping viruses. The defence system can't destroy them because antibodies and defence cells never enter body cells and completely ignore cells that are behaving normally.

Although herpes viruses do not seem to harm the nerve cell, there is one type that stays in the nerve cells just under the skin of the lips. In some people these viruses leave the nerves every so often and begin to attack the skin cells of the lips. This causes the blistery sore called a cold sore. Scientists don't know what makes the herpes viruses suddenly begin to attack. These sores often occur just after a cold or when a person is worried or upset, for instance, during school examinations. Cold sores also seem to run in families. Obviously there are many factors involved.

Scientists have not developed a way of curing cold sores completely. But there is a medicine that can make a cold sore go away if it is put on just as the blister is beginning to form. Some doctors have found that holding an ice cube on the sore as it begins to form also makes it go away. But, as this takes several hours, it would probably cause more discomfort than it prevents. Eventually the defence system gets rid of the viruses and the sore is repaired, but there still are more herpes viruses in the nerve cells.

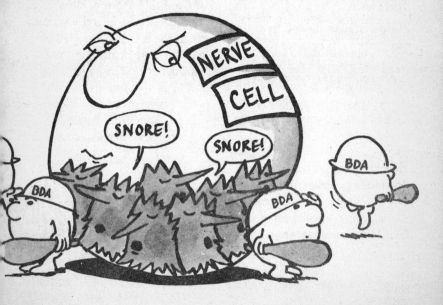

Some other diseases caused by viruses

Each type of virus attacks in a slightly different way and in a slightly different part of the body. But since fever and inflammation are two of the ways the body fights viruses, most virus infections have these symptoms.

The mumps viruses reproduce inside the cells of some types of glands, especially those in the neck that make saliva (salivary glands) for the mouth. So, when you have mumps, these glands swell up and get sore. Some people don't become completely immune to the mumps virus after one attack and may get mumps again. But hardly anyone gets them more than twice.

Polio is a virus disease that can cause paralysis because it reproduces inside some of the nerve cells in the spine. The virus sometimes damages the nerves permanently and, after people recover from the disease, they may still be unable to use some parts of their body. They may be unable to walk or have trouble breathing. Fortunately few people get polio any more because vaccines have been developed against it.

The viruses that cause rabies attack many nerve cells in the brain and spine. This causes the person or animal who has rabies to act strangely and eventually it causes death, if it isn't treated quickly. Rabies is usually spread when an infected animal bites a healthy one because rabies viruses grow in salivary glands and are released into the saliva. The saliva gets into the wound from the bite and the viruses pass into the healthy animal's blood.

Warts

Warts are not caused by toads. They are caused by viruses that work in a very different way from cold and flu viruses. They enter the cells that are just under the skin and start to change the way the cells work.

①

As well as making the cells start producing more viruses, they make the cells change their shape. The virus-infected cells grow into a lump. This, of course, is the wart.

Wart viruses don't reproduce quickly and spread around the body, and the warts themselves stop growing after they reach a certain size. The viruses don't injure the cells so the defence system isn't alerted and doesn't try to destroy the viruses and the cells they've taken over. This is why warts aren't painful unless they are in an inconvenient place such as the sole of your foot.

Getting rid of warts is quite difficult and is best done with the help of a doctor. There are chemicals that can be painted on top of the wart that kill the cells. These don't always work though, because they often can't reach all the cells in the wart.

Another way of killing wart cells is freezing them. Sometimes the doctor will give an injection that prevents you from feeling anything in the area of the wart. Then he will simply cut the wart off. But lots of times the wart will just suddenly go away by itself when you least expect it.

Infection by bacteria

Bacteria are generally much more dangerous than viruses. A cut or sore throat that has become infected with bacteria can cause damage to the whole body. Many bacteria release harmful poisons into the blood and tissues. If they're given the chance, bacteria will multiply and spread all over the body. For thousands of years many people, especially children, died of bacterial infections. But today things are very different. Bacteria are a bother and often cause problems but, if the infections are given proper medical care, they seldom cause death.

This change began about a hundred years ago when scientists discovered that tiny invisible organisms cause infections and that, by preventing these organisms from entering the body, infections can be prevented.

Doctors found that if they washed a cut and kept it clean, the cut seldom got infected.

They also learned that faeces, the solid waste that comes from the body, contain millions of bacteria. (This is why it's a good idea to wash your hands after going to the toilet.) The bacteria live in the large intestine or colon and seem to help with the final digestion of food. Most of them are quite harmless as long as they stay in the colon but, if they escape into the rest of the body, they can be very dangerous. This is what can happen if a person with appendicitis doesn't have an operation in time (see page 40).

In the past, before people understood how dangerous the bacteria in faeces are, sewage often polluted the water supply.

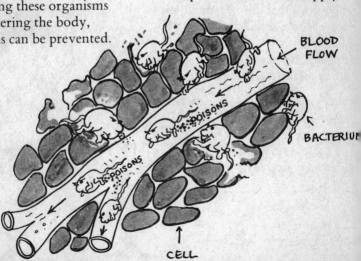

BLOOD FLOW

POISONS

POISONS

BACTERIUM

CELL

If someone had an infection it would often spread around the town. Even today, the people in many parts of the world are too poor to build toilets and sewers so disease is more common there than it is in rich countries.

There have been two more medical discoveries that have reduced even more the risk of bacterial infection in both rich countries and poor countries. The first was vaccination (see page 14). The second was the discovery of medicines such as penicillin and tetracycline. These are called antibiotics and are chemicals that are safe for most humans to swallow – even in quite large doses – but they are deadly for bacteria.

Antibiotics weaken or kill most of the bacteria inside the body of the person who takes them.

Even if you have a bad bacterial infection, a course of antibiotics will usually clear it up in a few days. It stops the bacteria multiplying and gives your defence system a chance to get rid of them. Usually you will start to feel better about a day after you start taking antibiotics. But just because you're feeling better, it doesn't mean the infection has cleared up completely. It is important to keep taking the antibiotics the doctor gives you until they are all gone. By this time the bacteria are usually all gone as well.

WE DON'T STAND MUCH CHANCE – HE'S WASHING THE CUT!

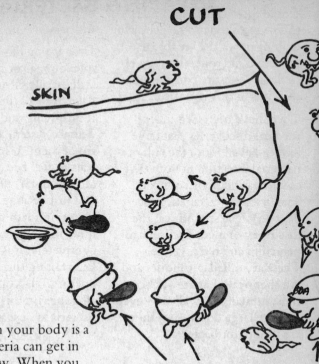

CUT

SKIN

BODY DEFENCE

Every opening in your body is a place where bacteria can get in and begin to grow. When you cut yourself, it gives them a new way in. A cut that is badly infected is more angry and painful than a clean cut. It takes longer to heal and is more likely to leave a scar. This is because the bacteria inside the cut are making chemicals that cause extra damage to the injured place.

Small but deep cuts (like the kind you'd get if you stood on a nail while wearing soft shoes) are the most likely to become infected. Even if you wash such a wound very carefully, you may not get rid of all the bacteria. It is a good idea to

show this sort of cut to a doctor, even if it doesn't seem too bad. You may need antibiotics. The wound from an animal bite ought to be seen by a doctor too, especially if there is a chance the animal has rabies.

If you cut yourself while in a stable or pasture, or even in a garden that has been fertilized with manure, there is a risk of being infected with a particularly dangerous type of bacteria. These bacteria

INVADING BACTERIA

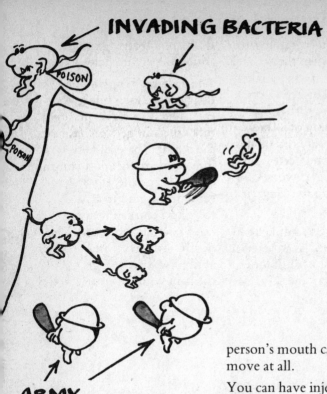

ARMY

normally live in the intestines of cattle and horses but, if they begin to grow in humans, they produce a dangerous disease called tetanus. As they grow, these bacteria release a poison into the blood. If a person with this infection doesn't receive treatment, the poison will build up in his body and after a few days his muscles will become stiff and he will have trouble opening his mouth. The infection is sometimes called lockjaw because eventually the person's mouth can hardly move at all.

You can have injections (or "shots") to make you immune to the poisonous chemical made by the tetanus bacteria. Most people begin to have them when they are babies. The immunity to tetanus begins to weaken after a time so it is a good idea to have a tetanus booster shot every few years, especially if you ride horses or live on a farm. If you cut yourself when you are near horse or cow manure or in any dry dusty place, it is best to see a doctor, If you haven't had a tetanus shot in the past year, the doctor may give you one, just to be on the safe side.

27

Sore throat and ear-ache

Like viruses, bacteria can live in the throat and, when they increase in number, they make the throat sore. This feels very much like the sore throat you get at the beginning of a cold. Most sore throats are caused by viruses and soon get better. But, if the sore throat gets worse and lasts for more than two days, it may be caused by bacteria.

A doctor can take a sample from the throat to see if it is a bacterial infection and, if it is, antibiotics will clear it up very quickly. If it is a virus infection though, antibiotics are no help at all.

The bacteria living in your throat sometimes infect your ears. They can travel up small tubes that connect each ear with the throat. These bacterial infections are the most common cause of ear-ache. If you have a sore throat and ear-ache together, you can be quite sure it is a bacterial infection. The doctor will give you a course of antibiotics that will get rid of the pain within a couple of days.

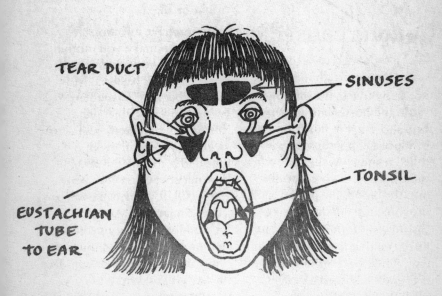

TEAR DUCT

SINUSES

EUSTACHIAN TUBE TO EAR

TONSIL

Tonsillitis

If you have a sore throat that keeps coming back again and again, it may be because you have tonsillitis. The tonsils' job is to produce chemicals that fight infection in the throat, but sometimes they can become infected themselves.

Food may get trapped in the tiny openings leading out of the tonsils. Bacteria that begin to eat the food may soon begin to eat your tonsils. Antibiotics usually get rid of the bacteria but, if you don't take antibiotics or if you don't take all the tablets as the doctor says, the bacteria may keep growing until they damage the tonsils so much that they must be removed.

A few years ago lots of children had operations to have their tonsils removed. But now doctors know that tonsils are an important part of the body's defence against throat infections. Today they always try to cure the infection with antibiotics and remove the tonsils only if they are badly damaged.

Coughs caused by bacteria

Whooping cough used to be a very common childhood disease like chicken pox, but now most people are given a whooping-cough vaccination when they are very young. Some people still get whooping cough, even after being vaccinated, but they only have a mild attack.

The disease is caused by a type of bacteria that lives in the lungs. These bacteria irritate the lungs and cause such a violent cough that it is difficult to breathe. When a person with whooping cough is in the middle of a fit of coughing, he often makes a long gasping noise when he tries to breathe in. This noise is called the whoop. Whooping-cough bacteria not only damage the lungs, they release poisons into the blood which cause a fever and make the person feel sick.

They cannot be killed quickly by antibiotics like most disease-causing bacteria, so antibiotics can't cure whooping cough. But the body's defence system usually manages to get rid of the bacteria in about four to six weeks.

Tuberculosis (TB for short) and most cases of pneumonia are caused by other sorts of bacteria that invade the lungs. They also cause coughing and fever and are often much worse than whooping cough. Luckily pneumonia can usually be cured quite quickly by antibiotics.

TB takes a longer time to heal, but today few people catch it. This is because there are skin tests and chest X-rays which show doctors who has TB. If a person does catch TB, he is put in hospital before the disease gets too serious and before many people have had a chance to catch TB from him. Cows can get TB too and, if they do, the bacteria may get in the milk. But today most countries require farmers to have all their cattle tested to make sure they aren't carrying TB.

Pasteurized milk is another guard against TB and other diseases that could be caused by bacteria in milk. The milk is pasteurized at the dairy before it is put into bottles. It is heated for a few moments to kill any dangerous bacteria. This doesn't kill all the bacteria in the milk. The kind that make milk go sour are still there, but these don't harm our bodies. To kill all the bacteria in milk means sterilizing it and this changes its taste quite a bit.

Boils and pimples

There are thousands of tiny holes in the skin, so small that they can only be seen with a microscope. Hair grows out of some of these openings. Some contain cells that make oil to keep the skin and hair soft and in good condition. Other holes contain cells that release perspiration to keep the body cool.

Even though the holes in the skin are very small, they are many hundred times larger than a bacterium. And, just like all the other openings in the body, they can become infected.

When this happens, a spot called a pimple forms. If the spot is very large and angry it is called a boil and, if it occurs on the eyelid, it is called a stye.

It is impossible to prevent bacteria from getting into the holes in the skin. They are there all the time. But they don't cause any harm until they begin to multiply, and they don't begin to multiply unless they have food. If an opening in your skin contains enough food to get the bacteria started, they begin to make chemicals that hurt your skin cells. This gets the

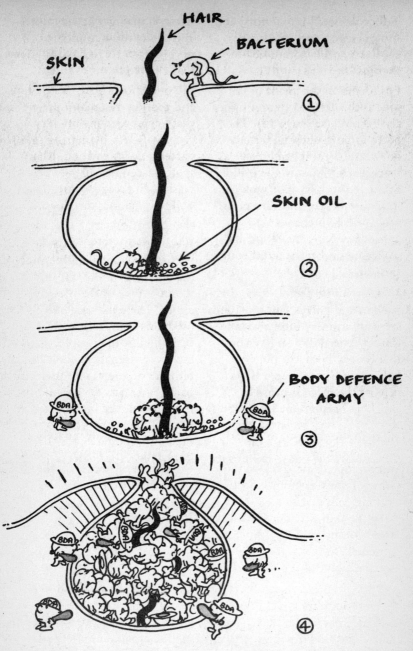

FORMATION OF A BOIL

body's defence system working. The skin surrounding the hole swells up to a hard bump and becomes red and painful.

Pus forms on the inside of the spot as the defence system fights the bacteria (see page 12). The body often pushes the pus up out of the spot. It can be seen as a small white spot in the middle of the red spot. A spot won't heal completely until this pus is removed. Sometimes it is carried away by the blood and sometimes it breaks out through the skin.

Usually a pimple goes away by itself in a few days, but boils and styes are more painful and take longer to heal. If you have one that is very bothersome, you can help it get better sooner if you can get the pus out more quickly. This is done by soaking the boil in very warm water or putting a hot wet cloth on it. This draws the pus to the surface so it can break out more easily. This is best done with the help of a nurse or doctor who can see that all the pus is out.

No one knows how to stop boils and pimples but many people say that keeping your skin very clean will help by getting rid of bacteria and their food. Many spotty-faced teenagers who wash their face ten times a day will tell you that this doesn't always work.

Washing can't get rid of the bacteria that are already inside the openings in the skin and it won't get rid of their food either. These bacteria live on the oil that is made inside the openings. Some people, especially teenagers, have lots of pimples on their face, chest and back. Scientists have found that these people are making more skin oil than others do, so the openings in their skin contain lots of food for bacteria.

People with this problem can get treatment. Chemists' shops sell creams and special soaps for people with pimples, but they don't work for everybody. If you have very bothersome pimples, it is a good idea to see a doctor to find out what treatment is best. Every kind of treatment takes several months to work.

Many people believe that giving up chocolate and chips and eating salads and vegetables will help clear up spots. There is no scientific evidence to show that this is true. When someone reaches the age of nineteen or twenty, pimples usually clear up on their own, though the odd pimple may crop up once in a while.

Tooth decay

On the outside teeth are made of a hard stony material, but on the inside they are soft and contain living cells, blood vessels and nerves. Damage to the outside of the teeth can't be repaired like other parts of the body and only the baby teeth are replaced by new ones. So, if your teeth are broken in an accident or if they are damaged by bacteria, a dentist must do the repairs.

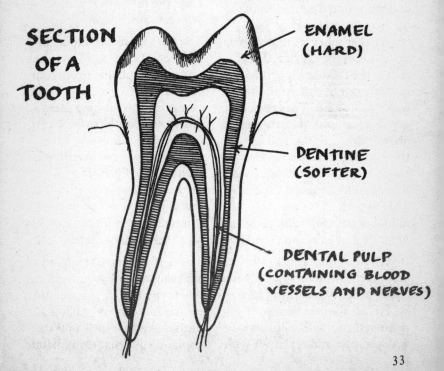

SECTION OF A TOOTH

ENAMEL (HARD)

DENTINE (SOFTER)

DENTAL PULP (CONTAINING BLOOD VESSELS AND NERVES)

There are many different types of bacteria in the mouth and most of them are quite harmless. They eat the tiny bits of food that get left in the mouth after we eat. Only one of them causes tooth decay. It is a kind of bacteria that lives in microscopic crevices on the surface of the teeth and forms a sticky coating on them called "plaque".

ACID →

As these bacteria eat and multiply they make acid which collects inside the crevices in the teeth and sometimes gets so strong that it begins to dissolve the walls of the crevice. This makes the crevice bigger. More bacteria can live there and they make more acid. The crevice gets bigger until, if the bacteria are not stopped, the acid eats through the hard part of the tooth and reaches the soft living tissue inside. This is what causes a tooth-ache. The infection damages the nerve and causes a great deal of pain and swelling.

If you go to the dentist twice a year you'll probably never get a tooth-ache. The dentist can see where the tooth is being dissolved and will drill away the decayed part and replace it with

a filling. Going to the dentist can be painful sometimes but it saves the pain of a tooth-ache which is much worse.

The way to stop tooth decay from beginning at all is to remove the plaque from your teeth about twice a day. This is best done by brushing them with a soft toothbrush. If you don't brush your teeth for a day or two they get covered with plaque. It is difficult to see because plaque is tooth coloured but you can feel it with your tongue. It feels as though every tooth has a furry coating.

To see if you have removed all the plaque from your teeth when you brush, you can use "disclosing tablets". These are pleasant-tasting little pills that contain a dye that turns plaque bright red. Chemists sell them but your dentist will probably give you some if you ask for them. After sucking a disclosing tablet you will probably find that some of your teeth are a bit red. This is because you haven't brushed away all the plaque in those spots. Disclosing tablets also turn your gums and tongue red. If you lick your lips when you have a disclosing tablet in your mouth, it will look as though you are wearing lipstick The red goes away in about an hour.

Another way to protect your teeth from decay is to eat less sugary food. Sugar is the favourite food of the bacteria that cause tooth decay and they grow much better in the mouths of people who eat lots of sweets.

Scientists are trying to find a way of giving people a vaccination against tooth decay. They are also experimenting with putting a plastic coating on teeth. But for most people, careful cleaning is enough to prevent the bacteria causing too much damage to teeth.

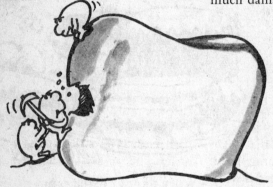

Using tooth-paste when you brush may help to clean the teeth slightly and many people feel it makes their mouth taste better, but it isn't really necessary. Some types of toothpaste contain a chemical called fluoride and in some places the water contains fluoride. Fluoride slows down tooth decay because it helps teeth resist the acid made by the bacteria.

Vomiting

Being sick (or vomiting) is a horrible experience. It makes you feel weak and shaky. It leaves a terrible taste in your mouth and it is often very embarrassing.

After food is swallowed, it goes down into the stomach where it is broken up into a mush. Chemicals are added to it that make the bits of food dissolve so they can be absorbed by the blood. It is these chemicals that make food taste and smell so awful once it's been in the stomach.

sick and some people, especially children, seem to get sick for no reason at all. Scientists are still trying to find out why.

Actually vomiting isn't controlled by the stomach at all, but by the brain – one of the automatic parts of the brain.

There are many things that make people vomit. Eating food that has been contaminated with some types of bacteria can make you sick. So can eating too much rich food. But very often the things that make people sick have nothing to do with eating or the stomach.

Many people get sick on long coach journeys or boat trips. Diseases like whooping cough can make you sick and many people feel sick when they are very frightened or worried. Seeing someone else being sick is enough to make some people

When this part of the brain decides that the stomach ought to vomit, it signals the muscles in the digestive system. Normally these muscles keep the food travelling the right way. They keep food from trickling out of your stomach and into your mouth when you stand on your head. (They even make it possible to eat while standing on your head.) When you are about to vomit, these muscles stop working and you have that horrible I'm-going-to-

STOMACH OLD WOULD YOU MIND SICK, PLEASE?

be-sick feeling. Then another signal from the brain tells a sheet of muscles called the diaphragm to begin to push against the stomach. This squeezes the food out of the stomach and up into the mouth.

What it is that makes the brain decide to make you vomit is still a bit of a mystery. Sometimes when you are sick it's easy to work out why. If you have eaten something that could be dangerous or if you have overloaded your digestive system with rich fatty food, it is important to empty the stomach. If you get something caught in your throat, you must sometimes vomit to get rid of it.

Some scientists believe that people get sick on rocky boats and rough roads because their brain gets a bit confused. The eyes and legs tell it that the body is sitting perfectly still, but other sense organs say that the body is moving. Many people who get car sick say they feel all right as long as they can look out of the window. Perhaps this is because the eyes are helping the brain to understand what's going on.

Scientists still don't really understand how or why sitting exams or taking part in a play should make people feel sick, or why just thinking about something unpleasant can make a person's stomach feel strange.

37

Hiccups

Scientists aren't sure why or how people get hiccups either, but they do know what is happening when a person hiccups. The diaphragm, that sheet of muscles near the stomach, is twitching. It is as if it is trying to push the stomach and make it vomit but can't quite manage. Eating quickly and laughing a lot often seem to cause hiccups, but sometimes they seem to start for no reason at all.

Hic!

There are many cures suggested for hiccups, such as holding your breath, drinking water upside down or breathing into a paper bag, but they don't always work. Some people have had the hiccups for months – even years! These people sometimes need to have an operation. This prevents them from ever hiccupping again.

Constipation and diarrhoea

After the food leaves the stomach, it travels through a curvy tube about six metres long called the small intestine. The food has been broken up and mixed with water in the stomach, so by now it is like watery soup and often gurgles as it travels along. The blood absorbs all the goodness from the food as it goes through the small intestine.

When it has finished, only the parts of the food that the body cannot use are left. Once the water has been removed from this waste, it is ready to leave the body as faeces. The blood absorbs the water from the reject food as it travels through another tube called the large intestine or colon. There are muscles in the walls of the colon that squeeze and push the reject food along.

If the muscles push very quickly, there is not much time for the blood to absorb water so the faeces are very watery when they come out. This is diarrhoea. If the muscles push slowly, lots of water is absorbed. The faeces become very small and hard and sometimes stop moving altogether. This is constipation.

Diarrhoea is often caused by chemicals which irritate the muscles in the colon and make them move too quickly. Sometimes these chemicals are in food and sometimes bacteria living in the large intestine make them. If you get diarrhoea, it is good to stay near a toilet for a day, eating and drinking a bit if you feel like it. Usually the body can get rid of chemicals or bacteria that cause diarrhoea in less than a day.

There are medicines that can quieten down the muscles of the colon if the diarrhoea is bad. But if it is very bad or if it lasts longer than a day, it is good to see a doctor.

There are lots of different kinds of medicine called laxatives that end constipation by getting the muscles of the colon to push faster. But people hardly ever really need laxatives because constipation isn't very serious and usually gets better by itself in a few days. If a person takes laxatives too often, they can, in the long run, make constipation worse.

Eating food such as brown bread and green vegetables which contain a substance people call "roughage" or "fibre" is the best way to prevent constipation. Roughage can't be used by the body so, if you eat lots of it, there is plenty of reject food in the colon. This makes it easier for the muscles of the colon to push at the correct speed. It also exercises the muscles and keeps them in good form.

Appendicitis

Once the blood has absorbed the water from the reject food, everything that remains leaves the body and is flushed down the toilet. But even though this left-over food is no good for us, it is very nutritious food for some types of bacteria. Millions of bacteria live in the colon digesting and absorbing reject food and multiplying very quickly. Many scientists believe that these bacteria are helping us in some way. They may be necessary for the final stages of digestion or they might be making vitamins that we need.

Rapidly multiplying bacteria are usually very dangerous, but the bacteria in the colon don't get out of control because every time reject food leaves the body, so do millions of bacteria.

The appendix is a small tube, closed at one end and attached to the colon at the other end. It too is filled with bacteria.

Sometimes the opening connecting the appendix to the colon gets blocked. When this happens, no bacteria can get out of the appendix and no reject

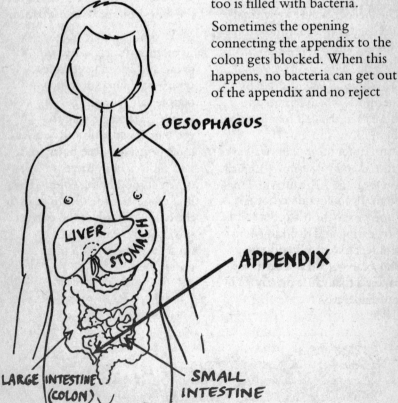

OESOPHAGUS

LIVER

STOMACH

APPENDIX

LARGE INTESTINE (COLON)

SMALL INTESTINE

food can get in. The bacteria trapped in the appendix keep multiplying until they run out of food. Then they begin to eat the appendix. This causes a great deal of pain in the lower right-hand side of the abdomen. If you have a pain like this, you must see a doctor to see if it is caused by appendicitis.

If it is, you must have an operation to remove the infected appendix. If you don't, the bacteria could eat away at the appendix until they eat through it. Then they would escape into the rest of the body and kill you.

Removing the appendix is quite a common operation and people who have had their appendix removed don't miss it. The appendix doesn't seem to do anything useful in the body so taking it out doesn't cause any harm.

Damage and repair

Whenever you get bumped, grazed, burned or hurt in any way, some of the cells in your body are damaged or killed.

The injury is repaired by making new cells to replace the damaged ones and organizing the new cells to work together just like the old ones did. This process is always the same, no matter how the injury is caused or where it occurs.

Cells that have been injured behave just like cells that have been damaged by bacteria or viruses and they release chemical signals. Some of these chemicals trigger special nerve cells that make us feel pain (see *Aches, pains and itching*, page 44). This lets us know that we have been injured and whereabouts the injury is.

Other chemicals released by the damaged cells trigger the manufacture and release of similar substances by other cells in the area. These call in cells and chemicals of the defence system and signal the repair system to start work.

Many blood vessels are very small and delicate and most injuries will cause some of them to break. Blood leaks from the broken blood vessels into the injured area.

A small amount of bleeding is good, especially from an open wound because the blood washes the wound. But it must be stopped quite quickly, not only because blood is too valuable to lose, but because, if there is too much blood around, it interferes with healing.

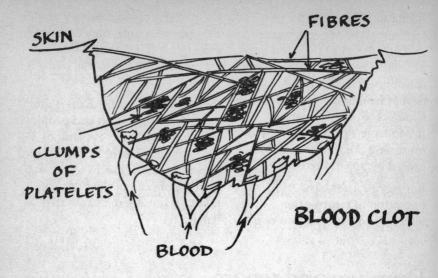

SKIN

FIBRES

CLUMPS
OF
PLATELETS

BLOOD

BLOOD CLOT

Stopping bleeding is seldom a big problem because the blood stops the bleeding itself. As soon as it leaks from a broken blood vessel, it begins to turn to a jelly and plugs up the leak. This is called blood clotting. Blood clots form because there are tiny cells in the blood called platelets that become sticky and clump together if they travel through a damaged blood vessel.

The clumps of platelets that form in broken blood vessels can sometimes plug the leak by themselves. If not, some chemicals in the blood join together to make very thin fibres that form a net over the wound. This net soon becomes plugged with platelets.

Some people have blood that doesn't clot properly. This means that they bleed much longer than normal and have to be very careful not to injure themselves. It is most commonly caused by a disease called haemophilia which occurs in some families. Usually only boys get this disease. There are now ways of helping these people but scientists are still trying to find a cure.

When the bleeding has stopped, the repair can begin. But before the area can be rebuilt, the body has to get rid of all the damaged cells and any bacteria or dirt that has fallen into the wound. Most of the actual clean-up is done by phagocytes. These are bigger than most cells and look like blobs. They slurp up the damaged cells, defence cells, bacteria and dirt.

The thick yellowish fluid called pus that you often see in infected wounds, boils and pimples is formed from the dead phagocytes and the debris they've picked up. Pus sometimes collects under the skin so that it can be removed from the body. Otherwise it is carried away in the blood to the liver and other parts of the body where it will be broken apart or dissolved.

New cells are the first requirement for rebuilding the damaged area. When some body cells are damaged, nearby cells of the same type can make replacements by simply growing bigger and dividing in two. There are also cells that can change types. When replacements are needed, they stop doing their normal jobs, go to the injured area and begin multiplying. They then turn into the cells that are needed. They can't turn into any sort of cell, but it is quite possible, for example, for a cell from muscle tissue to become a skin cell.

Once the replacement cells have been made, they have got to organize themselves into tissue. New blood vessels have to be built. Nerve cells have to grow back together. If the injury is an open wound, new layers of skin have to be formed. Scientists don't know how the new cells can organize themselves so well that they can rebuild the tissue almost perfectly But they are trying to find out how the repair system works so that they can help it along. They hope that someday it will be possible for a person to grow a new finger or whole new arm if his is badly damaged.

Aches, pains and itching

You may have heard people say we have five senses – seeing, hearing, feeling, tasting and smelling. Scientists now know that we have at least two more – one is the sense of balance and the other is the ability to feel pain. The sensation of pain is quite different from the other senses. There are special pain detectors all over the body that let us know when we are injured, and the information about the location and severity of the pain is carried to the brain on a special network of nerves.

People have been born who are unable to feel pain just as there are people born who can't see. They usually have many many injuries that are slow to heal. They are more likely to burn themselves because, although they can feel hot and cold, they can't tell whether or not something is hot enough to hurt them. They may sprain their ankle without even realizing it and then injure it some more by continuing to use it.

Pain also lets us know when something is wrong inside us. You can't see appendicitis and, if it wasn't for the pain, no one would be rushed to hospital in time for the operation.

Aches, pains and itches feel very different but they are brought about in much the same way. Cells are injured and they trigger the manufacture of special chemicals in the injured area. A small injury produces only a small amount of these chemicals and may cause no pain at all, but when the pain-causing chemicals reach a certain level, the pain detectors are triggered and news of the injury is carried to the brain. As you probably know, this sometimes happens very quickly. There are several different types of chemicals that make you feel pain and scientists now believe that the type of pain we feel depends on the type of pain-causing chemicals that are produced. Some make you feel a dull pain, others give a sharp burning feeling and some make you itch.

No one can deny the usefulness of pain as a warning of injury, but unfortunately the pain often persists long after we have been made well aware of the injury. This, as you know, can be very uncomfortable. Also some types of pain, headaches for example, seem to occur for no reason. They can be particularly difficult to get rid of because we don't know what's causing them.

Over the centuries people have spent a lot of time trying to get rid of pain and several types of medicines have been discovered that work reasonably well. But scientists are still studying these medicines to try to find out *how* and *why* they work. It is now known that some types of pain relievers, such as aspirin, work by slowing down the production of some of the chemicals that makes us feel pain.

Others appear to interfere with the pain detectors, the nerves that carry the pain sensation, and even the brain. But the perfect pain reliever still hasn't been found. Once inside the body, all the pain relievers do many other things beside relieve pain and they can be quite dangerous if they aren't used properly.

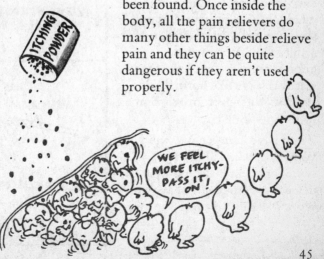

Cuts and grazes

When you get a cut or a graze, the skin cells, and perhaps the cells of the muscle and fat underneath, have been damaged.

When the bleeding has stopped, the blood clot dries out and forms a hard red scab. This protects the wounded area. The net of fibres in the clot then begins to shrink pulling the edges of the wound together.

If you remove the scab after about a week (this isn't a good idea if the scab isn't ready to come off by itself), you will see a thin layer of greyish skin over the cut. This has grown from the edges of the wound and joined in the middle. Later the cut shrinks and is covered by reddish pink, often shiny skin. The slight redness soon goes away, but often a scar remains where the skin was cut. It is not always possible for the repair system to make new tissue as good as the old. The skin of the scar won't tan like normal skin and hair will never grow from it.

If you have a cut, people will tell you to wash it. This is to remove dirt and bacteria so the defence system doesn't have to work so hard. An antiseptic may

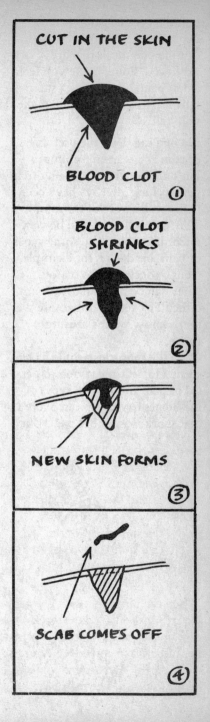

CUT IN THE SKIN

BLOOD CLOT

①

BLOOD CLOT SHRINKS

②

NEW SKIN FORMS

③

SCAB COMES OFF

④

also be put on the wound to help kill bacteria. But this unfortunately also damages your body cells. (That's why it stings). It is best not to put antiseptic right inside the wound.

When animals are injured, they lick their wounds and you may have noticed that many people, if they cut their finger, seem to pop it in their mouth automatically. This is actually quite a good idea because saliva will also help to clean the wound and kill bacteria. But it is a good idea to wash the wound before and after licking it.

Bandages are not always necessary but they are good for protecting scabs so that they don't come off too soon. If you get a bad cut, a doctor or nurse will stitch it up so the edges of the wound will be brought close together. This makes it easier for the wound to heal. You may also be given antibiotic medicine to help the defence system kill bacteria that may have entered through the wound.

Bumps and bruises

Bumps and bruises are caused by injuries that damage the tissue under the skin. A painful blow might not even show on the skin, but the pain shows that some damage has been done. As with most injuries, there is swelling and bleeding. When it occurs on a hard part of the body, the shin or head, the swelling is quite noticeable as a bump in the skin and is, of course, called a bump.

When the bump occurs on a soft part of the body, you often don't notice the swelling because it soon spreads out over a large area. But, after a while, a bruise appears. The purplish colour is caused by chemicals inside the red blood cells that have escaped from broken vessels and collected under the skin. Phagocytes soon begin to eat the blood cells and carry them away but it usually takes a few days to get rid of them completely. Sometimes bruises appear in the hard parts of the body after the bump has gone away. Usually they are quite small because there aren't many blood vessels in these parts.

Sometimes bruises seem to appear in the wrong place. If you bang your knee, you may find that your ankle has gone black and blue. This is because the blood from your knee has trickled down your leg to your ankle. This can also happen when you get a bang on the nose or head. You may find yourself with a black eye or two. There are many delicate blood vessels around the eyes and they are easily damaged by a bump on the face but, unless the eyes themselves are damaged, the body can usually repair the injury quite easily.

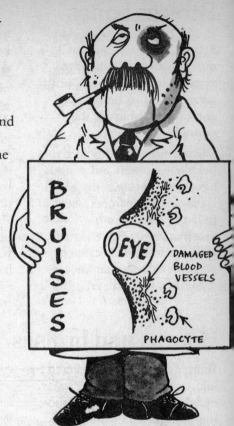

Nose bleeds

There are lots of very delicate blood vessels in the nose as well and many are very near the surface of the skin inside the nostrils. A bang on the nose often causes them to break. Sometimes even a change in temperature or weather can cause nose bleeds and sometimes they seem to start for no reason at all. But usually your nose will stop bleeding if you just hold it to keep the blood from running out. Don't tilt your head back

or the blood will begin to trickle down the back of your throat.

As soon as you keep the blood from running out, it gets a chance to clot and the clot will plug up the broken blood vessels. It will also probably plug your nose, but don't blow if for about half an hour after the bleeding has stopped. Usually by this time the breaks in the blood vessels have been closed.

Broken bones

Everyone who eats meat has seen bones. Bones don't look like living tissue – especially after they've been cooked – but the bones inside you contain living cells and blood vessels just like the rest of your body. Bones are held together by extremely tough cells that are all joined together to form a net called "connective tissue". Connective tissue is responsible for holding together many other parts of the body as well. In bones there are tiny crystals, like very small grains of sand, between the connective tissue cells. This is what makes bones hard.

Bones can bend a bit, but in some accidents the bones inside the arms or legs are forced to bend too much. Then the connective-tissue net is pulled apart and the bone breaks. Like any other injury a broken bone bleeds, swells up and hurts. Then it begins to repair itself. If the bone is badly broken, not simply cracked, the two broken ends are separated. Sometimes the broken ends even poke out of the skin. If a broken bone is to repair properly, the two broken ends must be fitted together.

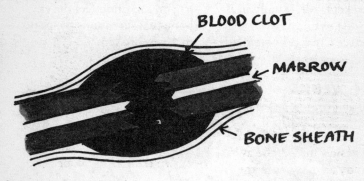

BLOOD CLOT

MARROW

BONE SHEATH

BONE BROKEN

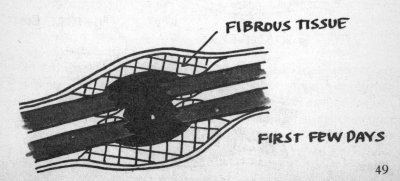

FIBROUS TISSUE

FIRST FEW DAYS

This is called "setting the fracture" and, since it hurts quite a bit, doctors usually do it while the injured person is asleep under anaesthetic.

Doctors take X-ray pictures of the broken bone to see how it is broken and to make sure it is setting properly. X-rays allow us to see bones because they can shine right through most body tissue and darken the photographic film that is placed underneath the X-ray table. But wherever there are bones, the photographic film stays clear because the X-rays can't pierce the crystals in the bones.

After the bone has been set, it must be kept still, usually in a plaster cast, while new connective-tissue cells are made to join the broken ends. Then bone crystals are laid down in the new net that is formed. The body always lays down too much bone tissue over the broken part and afterwards the excess is gradually removed in a "remodelling" process.

The time it takes for a bone to repair is different for each type of bone, each type of break and for each individual person, so doctors usually leave the cast on until they are quite sure the leg or arm can be used normally. Then they take an X-ray to be absolutely sure. The cast is usually removed long before the remodelling process is complete so you can often feel the extra bone that surrounds the part that was broken.

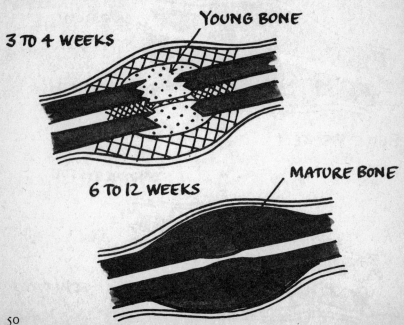

YOUNG BONE

3 TO 4 WEEKS

6 TO 12 WEEKS

MATURE BONE

Joint injuries

The places where bones are joined together are called joints. At each joint there is very strong connective tissue which holds the bones tightly together but lets them move. If the bones are moved too much or in the wrong direction, this connective tissue gets torn. It must be repaired before the joint can be used properly again.

Twisting the ankle, wrist, elbow or knee can cause this sort of injury. If it is quite bad, it is called a sprain and the injured joint must be kept still, even bandaged, until it is repaired. At the shoulder and hip is another sort of joint – a ball-and-socket joint. In some accidents the ball is pulled out of the socket as the connective tissue tears. This is called a dislocation. Before it can be repaired properly, the ball must go back into the socket.

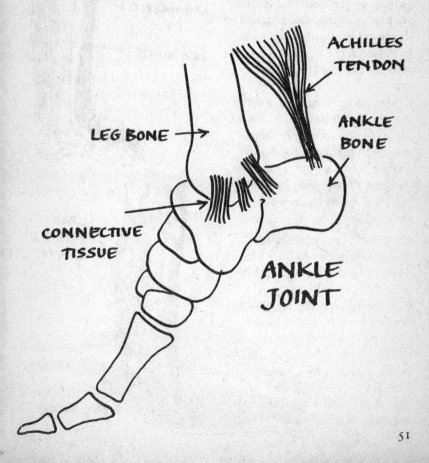

ACHILLES TENDON

LEG BONE

ANKLE BONE

CONNECTIVE TISSUE

ANKLE JOINT

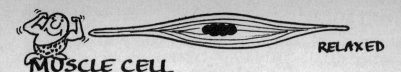

MUSCLE CELL

RELAXED

CONTRACTED

Muscle injuries

Muscles make joints bend by contracting (getting shorter and pulling on the bones). Muscles are held together and fastened to the bones by connective tissue. In between the connective-tissue cells are the muscle cells which actually do the contracting. Contracting takes quite a bit of energy and muscles need lots of blood vessels to supply their cells with plenty of food and oxygen. As they grow short of oxygen, they start to hurt a bit but they can keep on working for a while.

If a muscle gets very short of oxygen, it begins to hurt a lot. This is called a cramp. Cramps often happen when a person exercises shortly after a heavy meal. This is because blood is needed by the digestive system to absorb the food, so not so much gets to the exercising muscles. It also happens if a person is exercising while wearing tight clothes, especially

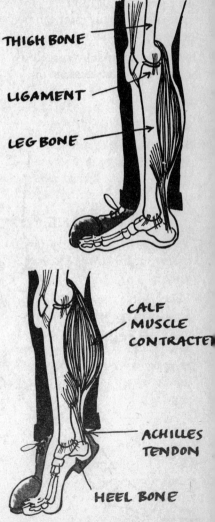

THIGH BONE

LIGAMENT

LEG BONE

CALF MUSCLE CONTRACTED

ACHILLES TENDON

HEEL BONE

tight underwear. They cause blocks and prevent some of the blood from reaching the muscles.

If you suddenly begin to work one muscle very hard, it often can't prepare itself fast enough. It may soon run out of oxygen and begin to hurt. Some doctors believe that this is why some people get a cramp in their leg when they stretch in the morning. The pain of the cramp is a warning that the muscle is short of oxygen and shouldn't be used for a while. To get rid of the cramp, you just have to stop using the muscle.

If you get a leg cramp in the morning, it may be because you pointed your toes hard when you stretched. Your calf muscle wasn't prepared for such hard work so early in the morning. To get rid of the pain, you must force your toes up and your heel down.

Some people get a pain in their side or "stitch" when they run. No one is quite sure what this is or what causes it. Some doctors believe it is a cramp, others think it is caused by connective tissue being stretched. Doctors do know that people are more likely to get a stitch if they run in cold weather, especially after a big meal. Getting stitches seems to run in families. In some families people get them very easily. In other families people never get them. Athletes have found that, if they do sit-ups and other exercises to strengthen the muscles of their abdomen, they will not get stitches so often. But it doesn't prevent them completely. No one knows how to cure a stitch either, but it usually goes away by itself when you stop running.

Another type of muscle injury is caused by making some of your muscles work much harder than they usually do. People who decide to try horseback riding or rowing for the first time on a sunny Sunday afternoon often suffer from these types of injuries on Monday morning. The overworked muscles hurt every time they are used. No one knows why making a muscle work harder than usual injures it, so we don't know how to help it get better. But it

does get better by itself in a few days. And if someone decides he likes horseback riding or rowing very much and begins to do it three or four times a week, his muscles will soon strengthen and they will no longer hurt the next day.

Muscle injury can also be caused by making the muscles stretch more than usual. If you can't touch your toes, it is because the muscles in the back of your leg and the connective tissue that holds them to the bones are too short to let you bend over that far. If one day you decide to touch your toes no matter how much it hurts, you will stretch the muscle cells and connective-tissue cells beyond their limit and some of them will be damaged. They usually hurt for a few days afterward as the injured cells are replaced. During this time, the muscle is even less stretchy than usual. But, if you keep trying to touch your toes, the muscle and connective tissue will eventually grow longer as they heal. Then touching your toes will no longer be a problem.

Sometimes if you fall and land in a rather strange position, you may stretch your muscles far too much. The injury that results is called a pulled muscle. It hurts more and takes longer to heal than a normal over-stretched muscle, but it is the same sort of injury.

Burns, scalds and too much sun

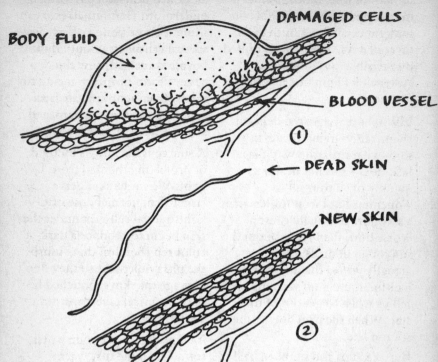

BODY FLUID

DAMAGED CELLS

BLOOD VESSEL

①

DEAD SKIN

NEW SKIN

②

If you have ever accidentally touched a hot iron or boiling water, you know how painful a burn or scald can be. The substances that make up living tissues are very delicate and they can be damaged if they get too hot. (An egg is made of the same sort of substances and look what happens to it when it is put in a frying pan!) A burn or scald sometimes just gets a bit red and soon gets better. This means that only the skin is damaged. If tissue under the skin is damaged, a blister forms. The watery substance inside a blister is body fluid that has seeped out of the damaged blood vessels. It stays just under the skin and, if the blister isn't broken, the blood vessels soak it up again in a day or two. It's best to try not to break a blister because it protects the burned area. If a blister is broken, the wound usually hurts more and it may get infected with bacteria. If you get a burn, you should run a gentle stream of cold water over it as soon as possible. This helps stop the pain and may lessen the damage. Putting ointment or butter on the burn doesn't help at all.

Sunburn looks and feels very similar to other burns, but it isn't caused by heat. Bright sunlight can cause a burn even on cool days. This burn is caused by invisible rays called "ultraviolet light" or UV light for short.

UV light damages the delicate chemicals in living tissues in somewhat the same way that heat does – but not nearly so quickly or so painfully. Touching a hot iron for less than a second will usually cause a worse burn than lying out in the sun for an hour. But since actually *getting* the sunburn isn't painful, there is no warning to tell us when to get out of the sun. When the pain does come it's too late.

Burns, scalds and sunburn heal in much the same way as other injuries. The body gets rid of the damaged tissue and new tissue grows. The outer layer of skin that has been burned comes off as soon as new skin has formed underneath. Sunburned skin can sometimes be peeled off in sheets several centimetres long. If the burn is quite bad, new skin cannot form properly and a scar is left. Even sunburn can cause scars, especially if the damaged skin is peeled off too soon.

A suntan is the body's method of protecting the skin from UV light. When the skin gets a larger than normal dose of UV light, special cells just under the skin begin to produce a dark-coloured chemical that absorbs the ultraviolet rays so they don't damage the skin so much. The dark chemical gives your skin the tan colour.

You probably get your worst sunburn on the first warm sunny days of the year, before the body has had a chance to prepare itself for the stronger sunshine of summer.

THEY HAVEN'T JOINED UP YET!

The countries of Northern Europe and Scandinavia have only limited sunshine. People whose families have lived in these areas for thousands of years usually have skin which isn't able to cope with too much UV light. Their skin contains few of the cells which produce the dark-coloured chemical that absorbs UV light, so they never get very brown and often suffer from sunburn. But people who come from countries nearer the Equator, where the sunlight is stronger, are usually darker and better protected. Many Africans have very dark skin all year round, but their skin still gets darker during the warm sunny time of the year

Some people, especially people with red hair, can get a suntan on some parts of their skin but not on others. This makes their skin get small brown patches called freckles. Each freckle contains the chemical which absorbs UV light and protects against sunburn. The skin between the freckles can burn though and, no matter how long a person with freckles stays out in the sun, his freckles will never join together and produce an even tan.

If you have pale skin and get sunburned easily, it is best to protect yourself from strong sunlight. But it isn't necessary to stay inside or wear lots of clothes all the time. There are special creams and oils to spread on the skin that contain chemicals that prevent UV light from reaching the skin and damaging it. They are usually called "suntan oils", even though they do nothing to help you get a suntan. Be sure to put suntan oil on every part of your body that is exposed to the sun. And remember that it washes off in water.

Allergies

Some people suddenly start sneezing, their noses start to run and their eyes to water. It is as if they have a cold, even though they feel quite healthy in every other way. Other people suddenly break out in nasty-looking itchy spots, even though they feel fine. If this happens to you, you are probably allergic to something.

Many people are allergic to some things and there are many, many different things that people can be allergic to. Dust, the pollen from plants, animal hair, drugs and some kinds of food are just a few of the substances that can trigger an allergy.

Allergies seem to be caused by some sort of mistake in the defence system. Normally strong defensive tactics are only used by the body when it is injured but, if a person has an allergy, his body fights against completely harmless substances as if they were causing a disease. That is why it causes many of the symptoms of a disease.

Scientists have found that people with allergies have antibodies in their blood that recognize the substance they are allergic to and mobilizes the defence system. This brings on sneezing, a rash or even makes a person faint or have asthma.

If you are bothered by strange symptoms that you think may be due to an allergy, you should see a doctor. The doctor can find out if it is an allergy and, if it is, what you are allergic to. The best way to prevent getting allergy symptoms is to avoid the thing you're allergic to.

ATCHOO!

ALLERGIC

If that is impossible (if the substance is around all the time like pollen or dust), you may need treatment.

There is a type of medicine called antihistamine that works against the defence system and quietens down the allergy symptoms. The doctor can also give you injections of tiny amounts of the substance to make your body become used to it.

Asthma

From time to time some people have attacks of not being able to breathe properly. They can't seem to breathe deeply enough. These attacks can last from half an hour to several hours. This is asthma. The attacks can be very frightening and getting frightened can often make them worse. Sometimes asthma is caused by an allergy and sometimes it has other causes which doctors don't understand yet.

There are medicines that can stop an asthma attack and allow a person to breathe properly again. Other medicines help prevent future attacks. They aren't a cure but they allow most people with asthma to live a normal life. Nearly half the children who have asthma get a lot better when they reach their teens.

REACTION

BEE STING

Insect bites and stings

An insect bite or sting usually leaves an injury that lasts for three or four days. It may only be a bothersome itchy bump, or it may be very painful and swollen.

Most insects are perfectly harmless, but there are a few different sorts that drink the blood of animals for food – mosquitoes and fleas are two examples. To get the blood they have to puncture a small hole in the animal's skin. This is usually a bit annoying. But many of them also inject a bit of their saliva into the hole to make it easier to suck out the blood.

The body's defence system recognises the saliva as foreign and rushes in to destroy it and make sure it doesn't spread round the body. This is what causes the redness, swelling and itching in the area that has been bitten.

Insects that sting like bees and wasps aren't interested in your blood at all. Their sting is very painful and is a warning to stop you from bothering them or their nests again. The insects aren't actually thinking all that out as they sting. They are just acting on instinct. But the warning works. Most people know very well that they ought to be careful with bees.

BLOOD VESSEL

A stinging insect punctures the skin and injects a chemical that causes pain. Scientists have found that many of these chemicals not only injure our cells, they can trigger our pain detectors directly. This makes us feel a lot of pain very suddenly.

Different people react to insect bites in different ways. Some people get huge annoying spots when a mosquito bites them. Other people don't even notice they have been bitten. Some beekeepers say they have become quite used to bee stings and that they don't cause much bother. But a few people have actually died from a bee-sting.

This difference is due to differences in people's defensive system. The harder the body fights against the chemicals injected by the insect, the worse the bite will be. There are some medicines that can help if a bite triggers a very strong defence reaction, but usually all you can do if you get bitten or stung is wait for a few days until the bite goes away by itself.

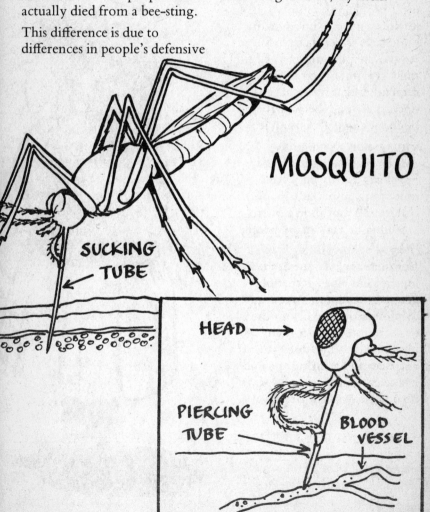

MOSQUITO

SUCKING TUBE

HEAD →

PIERCING TUBE

BLOOD VESSEL

Getting better

Illness and injuries are unpleasant but they are really a normal part of life. The human body is by no means indestructible, but it can protect and repair itself which is nearly as good. The body's defence and repair system can cope with most problems on its own. In a few cases it can't, but in many of these cases scientists have found ways of helping the body heal itself. It is important to remember that medicine and doctors are only helping the body, not actually curing it.

This book is about quite common ailments and these problems usually get better quite easily, especially in children. If they didn't, there wouldn't be very many people left.

But there are, of course, a few injuries and illnesses that never get better and sometimes cause death. Serious damage to the eyes can lead to permanent blindness. In some diseases, such as cancer and arthritis, the body just seems to go wrong – as yet no one knows how or why.

Living things are tremendously complicated and right now thousands of scientists all over the world are performing experiments designed to tell us more about how they work.

The things that make the body work properly are usually much more mysterious and interesting than the things that make it go wrong. Much of today's research may lead to ways of helping cure the diseases that are now very serious. But, just as important, it will make it possible for people to understand more about what's going on inside them.

Index